GIRL IN THE 419

ANKIT SINGH

BLUEROSE PUBLISHERS
India | U.K.

Copyright © Ankit Singh 2024

All rights reserved by author. No part of this publication may be reproduced, stored in a retrieval system or transmitted in any form or by any means, electronic, mechanical, photocopying, recording or otherwise, without the prior permission of the author. Although every precaution has been taken to verify the accuracy of the information contained herein, the publisher assumes no responsibility for any errors or omissions. No liability is assumed for damages that may result from the use of information contained within.

BlueRose Publishers takes no responsibility for any damages, losses, or liabilities that may arise from the use or misuse of the information, products, or services provided in this publication.

For permissions requests or inquiries regarding this publication, please contact:

BLUEROSE PUBLISHERS
www.BlueRoseONE.com
info@bluerosepublishers.com
+91 8882 898 898
+4407342408967

ISBN: 978-93-5989-065-4

Cover design: Ankit Singh
Typesetting: Rohit

First Edition: February 2024

Dedication

To Her,

In the tapestry of life, amidst the vivid hues of joy and sorrow, you have been my muse, my guiding star, and the silent anthem of my heart. These words, etched in the ink of my soul, are dedicated to you—the girl who has woven herself into the very fabric of my existence.

A decade has passed, a decade of unspoken love, silent confessions, and the quiet symphony of affection that has played in the theater of my heart. Each passing moment has only deepened my admiration for you, like the roots of a steadfast tree that endure both gentle breezes and raging storms.

You are the sunbeam that softly caresses my waking hours, the gentle rain that nourishes the garden of my dreams, and the moonlight that kisses my thoughts when darkness looms. Your laughter is the melody that orchestrates my joy, and your absence, the silent ache that accompanies solitude.

Through the pages of this book, I have bared my soul, allowing the ink to flow freely as my emotions take flight in verses. Every word penned here is a testament to the love that I have nurtured, albeit silently, throughout these years. The stanzas are woven from the delicate threads of my affection, fearlessly expressing the whispers of my heart, forever entangled with the thought of you.

Yet, fate has woven a complex tale, entwining our lives in a dance of destiny. And while I yearn to speak the words that have long been imprisoned within, I find solace in the fact that these poems, like a hidden bouquet, carry the fragrance of my love, reaching you in the ethereal spaces of literature.

In this tapestry of words, I strive to paint the portrait of my love, with brushstrokes of tenderness, hues of longing, and shades of devotion. It is a humble attempt to capture the essence of what my heart has held silently, to let my love breathe beyond the chambers of my soul.

You, dear reader, hold in your hands not just a book of poetry but a part of my very being—a confession and a celebration of a love that has whispered its presence in the corridors of time. As you read these verses, I invite you to glimpse the depths of my heart, to feel the emotions that have shaped my world, and to understand the love that has remained unspoken but profoundly felt.

May these poems echo in your heart, dear reader, and resonate with the beauty of unrequited love. For, in this dedication, the essence of love finds its voice, and in your reading, it finds a home.

With all my unspoken love, Ankit Singh

Acknowledgements

Gratitude is a symphony that resounds in the heart, a melody composed of countless notes of appreciation. As I stand on the threshold of this poetic journey, "The Girl in the 419," I am moved to acknowledge the souls that have graced my life and inspired this endeavor.

First and foremost, my profound thanks to the one who has been the beacon of my poetic odyssey, the silent inspiration behind these verses—the girl in the 419. Your presence in my life has been a guiding light, illuminating the path of my creativity. Though unspoken, our connection has been the cornerstone of these poetic musings.

To my family, my everlasting support, and the roots from which my aspirations have sprung. Your belief in me has been my pillar of strength, and your love, my unfailing muse. This book stands as a testament to your unwavering encouragement throughout this journey.

A heartfelt acknowledgment to my friends, who have been my companions in this poetic venture. Your camaraderie, insightful feedback, and shared passion for the art of words have fueled my creativity and sharpened my craft. Together, we have breathed life into the realm of poetry.

I extend my sincere appreciation to the literary community, the publishers, editors, and all those involved in the making of this book. Your dedication and expertise have ensured that my words find their place in the hearts of readers, for which I am truly grateful.

To the readers of "The Girl in the 419," you have breathed life into these poems, giving them wings to soar. Your appreciation and understanding of my emotions, my love, and my unspoken confessions mean the world to me. Thank you for letting my heart resonate with yours through these verses.

Lastly, but certainly not least, I bow to the universe—the boundless canvas that holds the brushstrokes of our lives. The trials and triumphs, the joys and sorrows—all have shaped me and this poetry. It is to the great tapestry of existence that I dedicate this humble offering.

In the end, what remains is my deepest gratitude—a tapestry of love and appreciation—for each thread that has contributed to this poetic quilt. May these words find a cozy nook in your hearts, dear readers, and warm you with the essence of unspoken love.

With gratitude and love, Ankit Singh

Foreword

In the delicate dance between heartbeats and poetic verses, love finds its most profound expression. It is within these rhythmic lines and mellifluous stanzas that the essence of "The Girl in the 419" is tenderly held. Allow me to lead you into this sanctuary of love, penned with utmost delicacy and heartfelt emotion by Ankit Singh.

As the pages of this enchanting book unfold, you will embark on a journey through time and emotions, guided by Ankit's skillful narrative. This collection is a testament to the endurance of love, the persistence of feelings unspoken, and the beauty of a love that defies the bounds of articulation.

In his earlier work, "Till the End of Time," Ankit Singh took us on a romantic voyage, painting love with vivid strokes. In "The Girl in the 419," he extends this journey, exploring the unvoiced longings and unspoken affections that have simmered over a decade. The number '419' encapsulates a decade's worth of love, growth, and longing—a room that holds a universe of emotions.

The beauty of Ankit's poetry lies in its exquisite simplicity. His words are carefully chosen, each syllable resonating with the heartbeat of a love unspoken. He employs metaphors that are both timeless and relatable, crafting a narrative that gently nudges at the strings of our hearts.

Through this book, Ankit invites us into the clandestine corridors of his soul, revealing the story of a love that has stood the test of time and circumstance. It is a tale that speaks of patience, the agony of silence, and the profound ache of unrequited love. His poems are a blend of longing and acceptance, a tender reflection of love's bittersweet dichotomy.

"The Girl in the 419" is not merely a collection of poems; it is a heartfelt confession, a love letter to the one who resides in Ankit's heart—a place known only to him and his muse. It is an invitation to delve into the depths of his emotions and resonate with the beauty of a love that has chosen silence over words.

As you turn the pages of this book, I encourage you to let Ankit Singh's words wash over you like a gentle tide, carrying you into the realms of love and longing. Allow the verses to caress your soul and remind you of the profound impact love leaves on the human heart. May this collection touch you as it has touched me, stirring the echoes of your own unspoken affections.

Prepare to be enamored, to feel the pangs of love, and to celebrate the enduring spirit of the heart. "The Girl in the 419" is a delicate dance of love, and I am honored to introduce you to this poetic love story.

Preface

In the realms of unspoken emotions and the whispers of the heart, there resides a story—a story that transcends words and finds solace in the poetic symphony of the soul. "The Girl in the 419" is not just a collection of poems; it is a heartfelt confession, an ode to love, and a tribute to a decade of emotions that have fluttered like delicate petals in the breeze of time.

This book, born from the depths of my heart, is a tribute to a love that has graced my existence for ten years. It is an offering to the girl who resides in my heart —a room that has held the echoes of my thoughts, the whispers of my dreams, and the fragments of my unspoken love. Though the words within may not reach her ears, they are an expression of the profound emotions that have etched themselves on the canvas of my soul.

As a poet, I believe in the power of words, in their ability to transcend the barriers of time and distance, and in their capacity to capture the ephemeral essence of love. Poetry, for me, is a language of the heart, a vessel through which I can pour the symphony of my emotions. In this collection, I have tried to infuse each verse with the tenderness of my feelings, the ache of longing, and the beauty of unrequited affection.

The number '419' holds a special place in my heart—it is a symbol of the decade-long journey that has shaped these poems. Within this number lies a chronicle of unvoiced confessions, silent conversations, and the passage of time. Each poem is a snapshot of a moment, a reflection of a feeling, and a silent prayer for a love that remains unspoken but profoundly felt.

The poems in this collection are an exploration of love in its myriad shades, a journey through the labyrinth of affection that has colored my life. They are an attempt to capture the beauty of longing, the sweetness of reminiscence, and the ache of unexpressed desire. I invite you, dear reader, to wander through these verses and immerse yourself in the emotions that inspired them.

To the girl who resides in the 419, may these poems serve as a whisper to the wind, carrying the essence of my love to you. And to the readers who share this journey with me, may you find echoes of your own unspoken emotions within these verses.

With love and sincerity, Ankit Singh

Contents

"Wish & miss" 1
"Love in Cyberspace: A Tale of 419" 3
"Yearning for 419: A Love Poem" 6
"Here You Are: A Proposal in Verse" 8
"Love's Melody: Every Scar, I'll Bleed" 10
"Unyielding Unity" 12
"Eternal Embrace" 14
"Arms of Everlasting Love" 16
"London Rendezvous: A Love Story on 419" 18
"Journey on Bus 419: A Decade's Love Unfolded" 20
"Innocence Unveiled: A Decade's longing for love" 22
"Journey of Love: From Tears to Stars" 24
"A Decade's Dance: Unveiling Love's Tale" 26
"Whispers of a Decade: Love Untold" 29
"Journey of 419: Love Across Lands" 31
"A Decade's Journey of Love" 33
"Forever Mine in Love's Light" 35
"Confessions at Dawn" 37
"Silent Echoes of Love" 39
"Boundless Love's Plea" 41
"Embrace of Eternal Dreams" 43

"Whispers of a Red attire Dance" 45
"Her, Only Her: A Symphony of Love" 47
"Eternal Friend: A Tale of Bittersweet Bonds" 49
"Incomplete Wishes: A Decade's Echo" 51
"Trusting in Love's Realm" 53
"Endless Love in Every Touch" 55
"In Your Embrace, Our Sweet Love Story" 57
"Embracing Eternity: A Love Unfurled" 59
"Eternal Hope: Love's flower Unfolds" 61
"Eternal Embrace: Love Beyond the Skies" 63
"Whispers of Maybe: Love's Eternal Promise" 65
"Boundless Embrace: A Love Beyond Time" 67
"Whispers of Devotion: A Dance Through Shadows" 69
"Eternal Embrace: A Symphony of Pink Hues" 71
"Nocturnal Embrace: A Love Unfading" 73
"Infinite Love: A Symphony Unspoken" 75
"Unseen Love: A Diamond in the Night" 78
"Endless Rhyme: A Love Beyond Time" 80
"Hearts in Eternity: A Tale of Transient Glory" 82
"Melodies of the Heart: A Ballad in Echoes of Love" 84
"Whispers of Love: Navigating the Winds of Fate" 86
"Whispers of Time: Love's Uncharted Journey" 88
"Eternal Patience: A Love That Transcends Time" 90
"Serenade of a Silent Love: Waiting Until the End of Time" ... 92
"Bound by Love, A Prayer for Tomorrow" 94
"Heart's Ballet: Longing in Silence" 96

"Mirror of Love: Fragrance Through Time" 98
"Echoes of Eternity: Love's echo Unveiled"...........................100
"Whispers of Eternal Love: A Tale Unveiled" 102
"Shadows of Love: Yearning for Forever"..............................104
"Decade of Devotion: Love's Timeless Journey" 106
"Endless Apology: Love's Redemption Song" 108
"Unyielding Love: A Promise Beyond Time" 110
"Love's Silent Vigil: A Decade of Waiting" 112
"Echoes of Love: Two Weeks After" 114
"Whispers of Forever: A Love Beyond Time".......................116
"Dreams Unveiled: In the Silence of Night"..........................118
"Endless Embrace: A Love That Transcends Time" 120
"Birthday Wishes: Love's Eternal Celebration" 122
"Enduring Echoes: A Love Beyond Time"...........................124
"Eternal Smiles: A Love that Transcends Time" 125
"Echoes of Strength: A Symphony of Shared Lives"..............127
"Love's Surrender: A Poetic Farewell" 129
"Love's Dawn: A Tapestry of Yearning"................................130
"Symphony of Solitude: A Love Etched in Time" 132
"Echoes of Love: Navigating the Tapestry of Time"...............134
"Eternal Threads: Love's Tapestry Unfolds" 136
"Starlit Serenade: Tales from the Night Drive".....................138
"Melody of Regret: A Love Unspoken" 140

"Wish & miss"

In the land of cyberspace, where connections intertwine,
A tale of love unfolded, like a dream so divine.
A girl in the 419, she captured my heart,
Her sweetness and wittiness, right from the start.

Her words danced upon the screen, like a gentle melody, Each message she sent, a piece of her mystery.
Her smile, oh so radiant, like the sun's golden glow,
Her voice, like velvet whispers, that made my heart's rhythm flow.

In every virtual encounter, I found solace and delight, Her presence, a beacon in the darkest of night.
For she was the one I longed for, the one I wished to keep,
Forever in my heart, even in the world of sleep.

Though distance kept us apart, our souls intertwined, Love knew no boundaries, in this digital design.
Through the pixels and bytes, our love did transcend, A love story unique, in this cybernetic blend.

I held her in my thoughts, even when we were apart, Her image etched within me, like a work of art.

She was the girl in the 419, the one who stole my heart, And I knew in that moment, we were never meant to part.

So let this poem be a testament to our love,

A bond forged through screens, guided from above. For she is the one I love, my heart's true desire, The girl in the 419, who set my soul on fire.

Forever her hand I want to hold,

As she is the one, combo of cute & bold

I wish my words could convince her someday, As this heart of mine, only with her always wanna stay

I always wanna tease her,like a small bug,

For her sadness when I see,I always want to hug..

Indeed this evening I still craved to hug and kiss, As I know the day I leave,it's all this mind..

And the heart which will miss...

I will miss the teasings,I'll miss our talks,

Our love is something forever which I want to lock..

And remembering the old days,I'll still say as my heart is keen,That, The girl in 419, where have you so far been...

"Love in Cyberspace:
A Tale of 419"

In the land of cyberspace, where connections intertwine,
A tale of love unfolded, like a dream so divine.
A girl in the 419, she captured my heart,
Her sweetness and wittiness, right from the start.

Her words danced upon the screen, like a gentle melody,
Each message she sent, a piece of her mystery.
Her smile, oh so radiant, like the sun's golden glow,
Her voice, like velvet whispers, that made my heart's rhythm flow.

In every virtual encounter, I found solace and delight,
Her presence, a beacon in the darkest of night.
For she was the one I longed for, the one I wished to keep,
Forever in my heart, even in the world of sleep.

Though distance kept us apart, our souls intertwined,
Love knew no boundaries, in this digital design.
Through the pixels and bytes, our love did transcend,
A love story unique, in this cybernetic blend.

I held her in my thoughts, even when we were apart,
Her image etched within me, like a work of art.
She was the girl in the 419, the one who stole my heart,
And I knew in that moment, we were never meant to part.

So let this poem be a testament to our love,
A bond forged through screens, guided from above.
For she is the one I love, my heart's true desire,
The girl in the 419, who set my soul on fire.

Forever her hand I want to hold,
As she is the one,combo of cute & bold
I wish my words could convince her someday,
As this heart of mine, only with her
always wanna stay

I always wanna tease her,like a small bug,
For her sadness when I see,I always want to hug..

Indeed this evening I still craved to hug and kiss,
As I know the day I leave,it's all this mind..
And the heart which will miss...

I will miss the teasings,I'll miss our talks,
Our love is something forever which I want to lock..

And remembering the old days,I'll still say as my heart is keen,That,

The girl in 419, where have you so far been...

"Yearning for 419:
A Love Poem"

In the realm of longing and dreams so true,
I yearn for the moment when our eyes will strike again...
For in my heart, there's a fire that burns,
Eager to meet my girl of 419, for whom my heart yearns.

She's the one I like, the one I adore,
The one who holds my heart forever.
Her presence, is a light in the darkest night,
Her smile, a ray of sunshine, a source of delight.

Oh, how I yearn to make her mine,
To cherish her love, forever divine
To cuddle in her warmth my heart thinks & shine
Together, embracing a love all so divine.

Hand in hand, we'll stroll by the shore,
Watching the waves dance, our spirits will soar.
With every step, will make talk our heart out,
Holding the cross hands,will click pictures with pout

Her laughter, a melody that lifts my soul,
In her embrace, I think am whole.
For she is the one I want to hold forever,
Wiping those tears which will not sit ever..

As the sun shines upon us, casting its golden glow,
I'll treasure each moment, letting our love flow.
For in her presence, I find my joy complete,
With her by my side, life feels, so sweet.

So, my girl of 419, know this to be true,
My love for you grows stronger, with every passing view.
Eagerly, I await the day fate brings us together,
To embrace your love, to create a love that will last long forever.

Am missing you more while watching every passing cloud,
I know wherever we'll meet,I can even find you
Within the crowd...

That smile which is different from the world which have everseen,
That's my only girl of 419...

"Here You Are:
A Proposal in Verse"

Here you are,
With all the struggles & all the hustles
Leaving all the run & leaving all the tears
Here you are...
& there is no dream of mine
To make u mine,
Rather i want you,
To make me urs
So that every morning,
I wake up and see your face
Within that flashing sun on ur face,
I want to stare you for those some moments
Where within my fingers i could feel the tenderness of your hair,
Those hairs covering that face so fair,
Waking next to which i want to spend my life,
Which has been so far, a little unfair,
And by placing those strands behinds your ears
I know in silence, i will definitely shed some tears,
But once those eyes of yours, will open & see,

Forever to be yours,its all i want to be

And wiping down my tears,

We will indeed fall in each others arms while losing that fear,

The fear which made us loose us, as being in the past,

Where the happiness and the smile used to forever last,

And remembering all those moments and unforgettable cherished scene,

I only want to ask,

That O girl of the 419, where have you so far been...

With these heartfelt words, my soul I bare,

From the beginning, until this very share,

I propose to you, my love so pure and true,

Please make me yours forever, for I Love you...

"Love's Melody:
Every Scar, I'll Bleed"

In tender embrace, love's seed is sown,
A symphony of care, affection's own.
With every breath, my heart will heed,
And with your every scar, I'll bleed.

Through darkest storms, we'll find our way,
Entwined as one, night turning to day.
In gentle touch, our souls will feed,
And with your every scar, I'll bleed.

Through trials faced and battles fought,
Together we'll conquer, love's strength uncaught.
In unity, our love will lead,
And with your every scar, I'll bleed.

For in your heart, my soul finds home,
A love that blooms and freely roams.
In every moment, a bond that's freed,
And with your every scar, I'll bleed.

So let us journey hand in hand,
Through life's rough terrain and shifting sand.
In love's embrace, our spirits freed,
And with your every scar, I'll bleed.

"Unyielding Unity"

Amidst shadows' grasp, don't let despair remain,
Unshackle the ache, the agony, the chain,
Beside you, I stand, to lighten heart's strain,
Hold my hand, united, let freedom regain.

Adorned with smiles, through daylight we'll sway,
In joy's tender grasp, troubles fade, melt away,
Bound eternally, our love's brilliant display,
Each passing second, my devotion's array.

Pain's burden, my dear heart, need not endure,
Within my embrace, find solace, be sure,
A haven where wounds find a gentle cure,
Love's flame ever bright, steadfast and pure.

Time will not steal this affection we share,
In unity, we conquer, a duo beyond compare,
With every heartbeat, you'll find me there,
Through life's winding journey, a love beyond compare.

Let not the shadows dictate the course,
For our love's strength is an unyielding force,
Together we'll conquer any trials, of course,
With love as our guide, we'll stay the course.

So, my dearest heart, heed these words I say,
Embrace the light that comes our way,
In each other's arms, we'll find our stay,
Forever and always, come what may..

"Eternal Embrace"

Through life's tempests, we'll find our way,
United, strong, we'll conquer, come what may,
In each other's arms, our fears allay,
Together, in love's warmth, we'll forever stay.

When dark clouds loom, and skies turn gray,
I'll be your shelter, a guiding ray,
With you, my love, I'll find my place,
In your embrace, a sweet solace I embrace.

Like a gentle breeze on a summer's eve,
My love for you, a melody that won't leave,
With every sunrise, our bond will weave,
A tapestry of love, in which we believe.

So, let go of pain, and doubts untold,
In my devotion, your heart will enfold,
With you beside me, I'll face the bold,
Together we'll journey, a story to be told.

In shadows deep, we'll seek the light,
Through life's trials, we'll hold on tight,
With laughter and love, our spirits ignite,
Forever entwined, like stars in the night.

"Arms of Everlasting Love"

And the day you feel my love,
Just find me and hug me,
Submerge yourself in my arms,
And I'll hold you close, endlessly.

In the comfort of our embrace,
All worries, we'll erase,
With whispered words, so tender,
Our souls will forever surrender.

I'll hug you back in charms,
A love that gently warms,
No distance can keep us apart,
For you are the beat of my heart.

I'll kiss you on your forehead,
A promise of love to be widespread,
With every touch, a healing balm,
To bring you peace, to keep you calm.

While wiping your tears and fears ahead,
Together, we'll face all that's unsaid,
With strength, we'll conquer any plight,
As we embrace the beauty of the night.

Under stars that shimmer and gleam,
You are my ever-lasting dream,
In this symphony of love's sweet art,
We'll dance together, heart to heart.

So, if ever you feel lost or blue,
Know that my love will guide you through,
For in each moment, come what may,
My arms are open, come what may.

"London Rendezvous:
A Love Story on 419"

Under that skies, our fates did entwine,
As you arrived,my heart raced, a moment divine.
That smile, so close, brought joy overdue,
Long lost happiness found, in colors anew.

Together we journeyed, on roads unexplored,
Laughter and gazes, a bond fully restored.
My eyes fixed on you, like stars in the night,
Your tears pained me, my sole wish: your light.

Thus, with love's intention, i thought to gift you a princess' delight,
I took the charge for bringing the smile,as an attorney,
To London's embrace, we took that journey.
The Bridge and the Big Ben witnessed our tale,
Walking together, I felt strong without fail.

Your face bathed in rays, radiant as morn,
Evening talks flowed till day was reborn.
In Tesla we rode, the chips disappeared,
Captured in spotlight, our memories revered.

Shopping and dinner, hand in hand we strayed,
In your peaceful sleep, all worries allayed.
Your snores a melody, a symphony sweet,
The face I cherish, a love so complete.

All through the night,my heart so race,
In the dark I did stared that beautiful face
May my affection reach you and touch your heart's core,
Into my arms, I pray my love,you'll explore.
With you the happiness blooms, no matter the day,
Together, forever, in love's gentle sway.
This is the love the sun and the moon always wanted to be seen,
O girl of 419, where have you so far been...

"Journey on Bus 419:
A Decade's Love Unfolded"

In a world of fleeting moments, she's my constant, my delight,
For a decade on bus 419, we shared dreams in twilight.
A girl I've known, a love that's grown, a bond forever tight,
Her presence warms my heart's abode, like a soft and gentle light.

Ten years have passed, a journey shared, each memory so sweet,
From youthful laughter to whispered dreams, our souls did often meet.
In that old bus, we found a trust, a love both pure and deep,
Her hand which i hope is mine, a touch divine, forever mine to keep.

I gaze into her sparkling eyes, a universe of grace,
In her embrace, all worries fade, time slows its frantic pace.
I long to hold her close to me, our hearts in perfect space,
To cherish every moment spent, as love's embrace we chase.

Her happiness my guiding star, I'd paint her skies with glee,
A symphony of laughter and joy, a love that's wild and free.
With every step, hand in hand, together we shall be,
Writing stories of forever love, beneath a destiny's tree.

Oh, the girl I've known for years, a treasure of my heart,
From bus 419 to endless shores, we'll never be apart.
I'll hold her close, our love's a rose, never shall we depart,
For she's the melody of my soul, the key to my own heart.

"Innocence Unveiled:
A Decade's longing for love"

In a world of wonder, she brightly shines,
Innocence graces her like delicate vines.
A girl who ponders, with eyes so pure,
Unravelling mysteries, seeking answers for sure.

Ten years have danced by, a decade's embrace,
Yet her why's and her smiles hold a timeless grace.
She walks through life with a curious heart,
Every puzzle she solves, a new piece of art.

Love, like a secret, I've held close within,
A treasure untold, yet my heart's voice does sing.
She's the puzzle I've cherished, my muse so dear,
Her laughter, her wonder, forever in my ear.

With a smile as bright as the morning sun,
She warms my soul like the day is begun.
Yet love's journey's complex, a path unexplored,
I stand by her side, my heart is assured.

Though she may not grasp the love I hold,
Her innocence a treasure, more precious than gold.
A decade of friendship, and still, I'm in awe,
A love that's grown deeper, without a flaw.

So I'll wait in the shadows, content to be near,
In her presence, I find solace, free from fear.
She's the why to my questions, the light of my days,
In her innocent gaze, my heart forever stays.

"Journey of Love:
From Tears to Stars"

Within the doors I saw her adore,
Searching for my eyes leaving that door,
Watching that smile,my heart skipped a beat
Like a queen I'll gift her happiness like a treat
She was welcomed with gifts,and the smiles
& talked about experiences covering the miles
She cried as her living wasn't arranged,
Tears were shed & in anger my mind changed
As for her happiness, I can buy the world
As for her smile I can travel the miles
Reaching to a decent place,she rested for a bit
Roaming in the evening, we gazed stars lit
We had a meal and listened a decent song,
Next to me she slept quietly,tired from the journey long,
With the next sun,we went to her small place,
During the journey I stared, the eyes I wanna chase
Stared the one whom I want to keep forever,
Taking all her worries,making her smile ever,
Seeming happy with the place, she laid onto her bed,
Remembering her family left behind,tears again she shed
Consoling her I made her very clear,

Now is the time to struggle, so remove all the fear,
She being the best will do everything good,
And I'll Continue to love her,always as I should
Leaving her for a day,I went ahead for my way,
She knew I'll be there for her, regardless of wherever she may stay
And with the calls we saw & heard each other out,
And still a lot of things in my heart, I want to tell her aloud
For her first day, she looked beautiful and so cute,
Guarding are her gods forever, while playing the rhythm on a flute
She was happy, and excited all for her first day,
Nervousness on her face and within all the things she say
I said everything will be fine and you will be all well,
Keep the focus on work and with mind do not dwell,
She was taken to her work with a person so unique,
Frustrating with journey & the anger at its peak
With the pain while walking , she dragged herself by someway,
Just her day should be well, thats all i had to pray,
Indeed she got drenched by the evening so hard,
But in the nightout walk she was again happy,
& so the smile and the laugh start
It's her whom I want to spend my life,
Keeping in my arms ,making as my wife
I'll take care of her,gifting all the happiness
And will make her smile, as many struggles till now she has seen,
But just tell me,O girl of 419,
where have you so far been...

"A Decade's Dance:
Unveiling Love's Tale"

In the realm of time, a decade's tale,
A girl I've known, a love unveiled.
Ten years of friendship, side by side,
Her presence a constant, my heart's guide.

Cute lips that curl in laughter's embrace,
A beautiful face, a vision of grace.
Chubby cheeks that beg a gentle touch,
Eyes that shimmer, emotions they clutch.

Long hair cascades like a silken stream,
In the sunlight's gleam, a radiant dream.
Sophistication, elegance in her stride,
Decency in dress, hearts can't hide.

Her allure goes beyond the mere exterior,
For her intelligence shines, ever superior.
Wit and humor, impeccable in grace,
A captivating soul, a cherished embrace.

From college days where friendships bloom,
A love unspoken began to consume.
Her essence, her being, a magnetic pull,
In my heart, emotions began to cull.

Time passed by, emotions did swell,
In the cocoon of friendship, love's tale did dwell.
A love that grew with each passing day,
Unveiling truths words couldn't convey.

For who she is, my heart beats strong,
In her presence, I truly belong.
A journey from friends to a love so true,
A story written in shades of me and you.

So here's to the girl with eyes that gleam,
Whose beauty is more than it may seem.
A decade's bond turned into amore,
Forever and always, my heart's own core.
I want to hug her submerging in my arms,
She has her own aura,surpassing all the charms,
& I'll Continue to love her silently in this way,
Gufting her smile,while taking the worries away,
Dreaming to walk in that slow breeze holding her gentle hand,
Love which will grow in a way,like a forever band,
She is an epitome of beauty which brightens up my sky,

Its my love for her which is the answer, of her thousand why.

She is cute and a beauty which i have never seen,

O my beautiful girl of 419,

Where have you so far been..

"Whispers of a Decade:
Love Untold"

In shadows cast by years of ten,
A tale of love, untold, again.
A friend of time, a heart so dear,
Whose beauty's grace brings joy so clear.

Cute and witty, a playful heart,
With honesty, a work of art.
Emotions flow like rivers deep,
In her, a treasure to forever keep.

Silent whispers of love I've known,
In secret chambers, they have grown.
Afraid to risk the bonds we share,
For fear that love might breed despair.

Ten years of laughter, tears, and more,
A friendship strong, a love to explore.
But words unsaid can tie us down,
And love unspoken, like a hidden crown.

Her eyes, a universe I've seen,
Her smile, a sunrise, golden and keen.
In every laugh, in every sigh,
My love for her soars high and high.

Yet the unknown path ahead does scare,
What if my words lead to despair?
I dream of a life with her by my side,
But fear of loss makes me want to hide.

In silent whispers, my love remains,
A symphony of heartache, joys, and pains.
For even if she never knows,
In my heart, my love still flows.

To risk it all, or let it be,
That choice is mine, the heartache, or glee.
But deep within, I'll always hold,
A love that's silent, yet so bold.
Its her beauty alike which i have never seen
And i ask her every time not to be super keen,
And my only question for her ,
Which has always been,
O girl of 419, where have you so far been..

"Journey of 419:
Love Across Lands"

On bus 419 we used to ride,
Side by side, our friendship tied.
Every day, a familiar face,
In the same route, a steady pace.

Ten years of memories we've amassed,
Through laughter, chats, and moments vast.
A connection bloomed as days went by,
Unseen feelings, like a hidden sky.

Today, in a car, in lands afar,
Destiny led us, a different star.
A new country, a foreign street,
Yet here we are, our souls still meet.

Surprise and joy, I can't believe,
By fate's design, we've both achieved,
To be together, a journey's quest,
In a foreign land, far from the rest.

Your smile, a beacon in the night,
Guiding me through life's twilight.
Ten years of friendship, now laid bare,
A love unspoken, a secret to share.

You're my confidant, my dearest friend,
With you, my heart will never bend.
The warmth you bring, the laughter true,
In every moment, I find a piece of you.

As we journey through this foreign land,
Hand in hand, we'll understand,
That distance can't tear our bond apart,
For you've always held my heart.

So here we are, in this new place,
Two souls entwined in love's embrace.
A decade's worth of memories to show,
And in this foreign land, our love will grow.

And many unspoken words i have still to say,
That ill always care for you, wherever you stay,
I want to hear your victories & challenges in the past you've seen,
As my heart still cant believe you are here next to me and asks,
O girl of 419, where have you so far been..

"A Decade's Journey of Love"

In the golden rays, side by side we'd stand,
Walking to the bus stop, hand in hand.
Crossing red lights without a care,
Seeking the bus, a vibrant pair.

"Is it orange or green?" we'd ponder aloud,
In the sea of buses, in the bustling crowd.
Amidst the sun's embrace, standing tall,
I'd steal glances, watching her worries fall.

Thirsty, she'd ask for water's grace,
At times fatigued, a tired trace.
I'd admire her beauty from the bus's aisle,
As she gazed out the window, with a distant smile.

Songs in her ears, a serenade,
By her side, memories were made.
In slumber, she'd whisper, a soft plea,
"Wake me when the bus halts, please."

In the throng, I'd guard her close,
Buying her ticket, was my work to choose
Every moment etched in heart's embrace,
A decade's worth of love's grace.

I dream to take her to a journey back in time,
Show her that past, precious and prime.
Reveal my affection through each scene,
A love that's enduring, pure, and serene.

She'll realize how vital she's been,
Through years that stretch, where love's unseen.
A decade's span, a cherished vow,
Forevermore, I hold her close, then and now.

"Forever Mine in Love's Light"

There's a girl whose presence is divine.
A desire burns strong, a love so true,
To make her forever mine, to cherish and woo.

With arms extended, I long to hold,
Embracing her tightly, a story unfold.
Hugging her long, a promise to keep,
In my warm embrace, her worries to sweep.

Wrapped in my love, she'll find solace and peace,
Her heart's every longing, I aim to appease.
A love that's enduring, steadfast, and strong,
Together we'll journey, where we both belong.

I'll be her shelter, her fortress, her guide,
Through life's ebb and flow, right by her side.
Her happiness, a treasure, I'll tirelessly seek,
With every sweet gesture, her joy will peak.

A smile on her lips, a glow in her eyes,
As I weave laughter and love, no goodbyes.
Forever she'll bask in affection's embrace,
A radiant joy, lighting up her face.

Through days that are sunny or clouded with gray,
I'll stand as her partner, come what may.
In warmth and in cold, in laughter and tears,
I'll be the constant in all of her years.

So let the stars witness, let the heavens declare,
A love so profound, beyond compare.
With hugs that reassure, and smiles that ignite,
I'll make her forever mine, in love's tender light.

"Confessions at Dawn"

In the dawn's tender light, at six o'clock's first gleam,
I confessed my love to my girl, the subject of my dream.
Ten years of knowing her, our friendship firmly tied,
In those moments of truth, my heart could not hide.

Her beauty, like the sunrise, a captivating sight,
Cute as a button, her smile shines so bright.
I poured out my heart, emotions laid bare,
Praying she'd feel the same, in that vulnerable air.

With bated breath, I waited, for her answer to unfold,
Hoping she'd say, "I love you," as my story she was told.
The day went by in whispers, like a slow, meandering stream,
Each moment felt like an eternity, chasing a hopeful dream.

She's the one I long for, the one who holds my heart,
My happiness resides in her, right from the very start.
For a lifetime together, I yearn to be by her side,
In her love and laughter, forever to confide.

As evening approached, my nerves were on the rise,
Anxiously waiting for her response, under darkening skies.
The sun began its descent, casting hues of gold and red,
I still hope that the answers should be yes,
Else this heart will cry with tears shred..

"Silent Echoes of Love"

And although the decision made me tore apart
As i loved her from the very start.
But still being near is all that i crave for,
Its my love for her,which is so brave for
& I do think of her,watching the night sky,

As yet in the depths of night, when stars align,
I dream of love, a future intertwined.
Her smile, her laughter, lights up my days,
But she remains a friend in countless ways.

Her stress, her pain, I long to chase away,
To see her thrive in each new light of day.
Her dreams, her goals, I'll always hold them dear,
And wipe away her each solitary tear.

I'll be her rock, her shield and forevermore,
Though love's confession lingers at the door.
I yearn for her to see what lies inside,
A love that's grown with time, cannot be denied.

I hope one day, she'll feel what I've concealed,
A love, a passion, that time has revealed.
But even if we stay in friendship's tether,
I'll cherish her, and love her, now and forever.

For in this tale, though love remains unsaid,
I'll be content to see her dreams widespread.
Her happiness, my heart will always heed,
A love, a friend, in every thought and deed.

"Boundless Love's Plea"

In your love, a boundless sea I've found,
Deeper than the depths, my heart is bound.
For your smile, I'd cross a thousand miles,
For your happiness, I'd go the extra aisle.

For every tear, I'd part the world apart,
To shield you from pain, I'd be the start.
For submerging your arms, I'd travel through the night,
With each gentle kiss, I'd bask in your light.

Forever, I wish you accept my plea,
To share this life, just you and me.
Holding your hand, my heart's complete,
With you, my love, my journey's sweet.

Though forever as a word, remains unclear,
While I breathe, I'll always hold you near.
In hope, I pray, our souls align,
As destiny weaves a love divine.

Underneath the stars, we'd find our place,
Two souls entwined in love's warm embrace.
The sky above knows my deepest truth,
The moon has witnessed the wait of our youth.

So, I'll wish upon those stars above,
For a love like ours, a timeless love.
In your arms, I'll forever stay,
No matter what comes, come what may.

For in your love, I've found my home,
Wherever we wander, wherever we roam.
Forever with you, my heart's decree,
In this love, we'll forever be free.

And dreaming about us being together,
I'll spend my lifetime as it has been,
Just tell me one thing,
O girl of 419, where have you so far been..

"Embrace of Eternal Dreams"

In the stillness of the night, they question my unrest,
"Why don't you sleep?" they ask, not knowing what's in my chest.
These eyes, yearn to linger, gazing deep and true,
Upon your lips, your nose, your cheeks, a radiant view.

Your forehead, like a canvas, where my heart desires to kiss,
And in the tendrils of your hair, my fingers long to twist.
Behind those ears, they'd softly slide, a gentle, tender grace,
As I lose myself within your eyes, a never-ending chase.

I crave to hold your hand, my love, and never let it go,
For in your touch, I find my peace, a love that continues to grow.
My arms, they ache to wrap around you, through the darkest night,
To keep you close, to feel your warmth, our souls taking flight.

Your waist, so slender, calls to me, a magnetic, binding force,
I yearn to pull you near to me, our hearts finding their course.
The warmth of your body, against mine, an embrace so sweet,
Two souls entwined, complete at last, as destiny we meet.

Your eyes, a window to your soul, I long to gently kiss,
As they speak my name, making it a melody of bliss.
Your cheeks, I'll kiss with promises, a love that will endure,
In every moment, forevermore, of this love so pure.

And in the embrace that binds us, heart to heart we'll say,
"My love for you is genuine, forever and every day."
In the quiet of the night, as stars above us gleam,
I'll cherish you, I'll love you, in this eternal dream.

"Whispers of a Red attire Dance"

In a dimly lit room, I chanced to behold,
A girl in a red top, a vision, untold.
As she danced with such grace, so carefree, so free,
My heart skipped a beat, for all eyes were on she.

Cute and beautiful, her smile was a treasure,
Elegance personified, in that fleeting moment's measure.
Her laughter filled the air, like a song in the night,
I watched in pure awe, lost in her radiant light.

With her friends she did sway, in a joyous array,
A tapestry of happiness, a sight to display.
I yearned to watch her, to capture that glance,
For she was a muse, in a mesmerizing dance.

Though my love is unspoken, a secret I bear,
She said no to my heart, a burden to bear.
Yet in this sweet memory, I find my release,
For loving her from afar, brings me a kind of peace.

She may never be mine, but I'll forever admire,
The girl in the red top, set my heart on fire.
In the realm of her dance, in the glow of her smile,
I'll cherish these moments, if only for a while.

So, I'll watch from the shadows, my love unconfessed,
For her happiness matters, above all the rest.
In the dance of her life, she deserves to be free,
And I'll love her in silence, for all eternity.

"Her, Only Her:
A Symphony of Love"

In shadows deep, where memories throng,
There walks a girl, whom I've known so long,
She's the one who makes my heart replete,
In her, my world's melody is complete.

With her, laughter's echo knows no bounds,
In her company, life's sweetest sounds,
Together we dream, explore and soar,
She's the one I'll cherish evermore.

A confidante, she holds my secrets tight,
In her gentle presence, my worries take flight,
She's the solace in my darkest rain,
The cure to every ache, every pain.

Her smile is the compass, my compass true,
In her eyes, I find skies of endless blue,
She's the one I truly care for, adore,
With her, I want to be forevermore.

In a tender kiss, our souls entwine,
In warm embrace, our love defines,
For in this world, under the golden sun,
It's her, only her, she's the only one.

With each passing day, our love has grown,
In her arms, I've found my home,
She's the star in my night, the radiant sun,
In this symphony of love, she's the only one.

In her, I've discovered life's sweetest art,
With her, I'll keep sharing my beating heart,
For in this tale of love, it has begun,
And it's her, only her, she's the only one.

"Eternal Friend:
A Tale of Bittersweet Bonds"

In the realm of love, a tale I'll weave,
Of a girl who's my strength, in whom I believe.
Her smile, my sunshine, my happiness untold,
But she longs for friendship, a love yet to unfold.

In her eyes, a world of mysteries reside,
A friendship, she says, with feelings she'll hide.
Her laughter, a melody, my heart's sweet song,
But the love I offer, she believes is wrong.

I'm a ship adrift, in her friendship's sea,
Navigating waters where love's denied me.
Yet, I'll cherish each moment, each glance, each touch,
For even as friends, I love her so much.

Her kindness, a beacon, in my darkest night,
Guiding me forward with its gentle light.
Though my heart desires more, I'll respect her plea,
For her friendship alone, is a treasure to me.

Through the seasons of life, we'll walk hand in hand,
In the warm, golden sand, or on rocky land.
Her friendship's a gift, I won't let it fade,
In her love or friendship, I'm truly unswayed.

For in her, I've found strength, a love so true,
Her happiness matters, whatever we do.
In this tale of a girl, my heart's bittersweet blend,
Her friendship, my solace, my eternal friend.

"Incomplete Wishes:
A Decade's Echo"

For a decade's span, I held a wish so dear,
To make it real, to chase away my fear.
But when it came to pass, my heart did fleet,
That long-awaited wish made me incomplete.

For in its granting, irony did enthrall,
I yearned for togetherness, but found the fall.
Alone, I stood, a solitary stone,
Drenched in my own tears, I sat alone.

I gazed out the window, lost in thought,
Of us, our past, the present, futures sought.
Complete and torn apart, my heart's cruel rhyme,
I longed to live with you one more time.

To cherish those moments, good times we have known,
To hold you close, not to be alone.
To gift you all I'd ever wanted, so sublime,
My love, affection, care, all in endless time.

Happiness unbound, a treasure to find,
So we could be together, entwined.
One more chance, a wish sublime,
To rewrite our tale, in endless time.

But dreams often fade, like stars at dawn,
And the chance for a second time now has gone.
Yet in my heart, our love shall ring like a chime,
A wish which will be left incomplete, for all of the time.
And still i will wish for you again in my next life
Untill i submerge you in my arms again,and could say,
How are you my beautiful wife ?
And watching us even the gods in the sky to u could say,
That its his arms, where you should forever stay,
And the world could have always stay and be seen,
By asking the question unlike me, that
O girl of 419, where have you so far been..

"Trusting in Love's Realm"

In the realm of "Us," we place our trust,
Two souls entwined, in love, we combust.
Together we stand, a formidable team,
Conquering life's challenges, it's not just a dream.

In the canvas of my mind, a vision takes flight,
You and I beneath the stars, in the tranquil night.
Your head on my chest, feeling your heartbeat,
With whispered words, love's symphony so sweet.

"I trust you," you say, with a smile on your face,
In each other's embrace, we've found our safe space.
We made it happen, against all the odds,
For the power of "Us" is a force sent by the gods.

On the steps of our haven, with tea in our hand,
We reminisce, laugh, and in memories we stand.
Far from the world's chaos, in our sacred dome,
Together we've built, a place we call home.

As evening descends, we share a meal so divine,
Bonds growing stronger, in the moonlight we shine.
A movie on the couch, ice cream in our care,
Love's simple pleasures, a connection so rare.

Upstairs, our bedroom, bathed in moon's gentle grace,
Two souls united, in a passionate embrace.
Kisses that linger, as time takes a pause,
In the language of love, we write our own laws.

Lips to neck, an intimate dance,
Our love, a fire, an eternal romance.
Bound by our spirits, hearts intertwined,
In this world of "Us," happiness we'll find.

Forever together, our souls interlace,
In the sanctuary of love, we've found our place.
Through life's winding journey, come what may,
In "Us," we trust, and together we'll stay.

So let this vision guide us, hand in hand we'll tread,
In the book of our love story, our tale shall be read.
For in the magic of "Us," we've discovered the way,
To make our happiness last, each and every day.

"Endless Love in Every Touch"

One day has passed, and I am missing her so,
Her soft touch, that smile, aglow in love's warm glow.
Cute reactions, long hugs, in dawn's first embrace,
Her radiant face, like the sun's gentle grace.

I watch that ring, upon her finger it gleams,
Those unsettled strands, through my fingers, like dreams.
I place my palm upon her brow, with a gentle wavy rhyme,
To make her feel I'm near, guarding all her fears in time.

I cross my hands upon her chest, holding her tight,
Grasping her closer, day and night.
Adrenaline rushes, when I smell beneath her neck,
Soft kisses placed, dearer with each peck.

Whether she believes or not, my love's pure and true,
Every single day, I'll cherish and pursue.
My heart attached to hers, in those tender hugs,
I'll make her see, I'm the one who forever tugs.

Love deeper than oceans, brighter than the sun's shine,
I'm her constant & her love forever mine.
Hand in hand, I feel complete and whole,
Together through all, our love's eternal goal.

In this world so dirty, my love remains pure,
I'll love her endlessly, that's for sure.
Till the end of time, my promise forever stands,
That I'll love her forever, holding her hand in my hands.

"In Your Embrace,
Our Sweet Love Story"

In your presence, I find bliss, you are near me,
A love so deep, a bond that's meant to be.
With every breath, you're by my side, you are,
In your embrace, I travel near and far.

So much I feel you, your heart and soul so true,
In this love we share, I've found my missing cue.
You are, for me, a shining guiding star,
In your light, I've found who we truly are.

I've lost myself to you, and yet I've won,
In this game of love, our hearts are as one.
From anywhere to anywhere, we'll roam,
With you, my love, I've found my truest home.

Let's go, my love, with no rhyme or reason,
Our love knows no bounds, in every season.
Without asking anyone, we shall meet,
Our love story, darling, is oh so sweet.

No barriers left to keep us apart,
We'll conquer the world, hand in hand & heart to heart.
And if the world tries to snatch you away,
I'll fight for our love, come what may.
Although you are my only win and my loss,
You're the decision maker & the cost

But for now, you're here, in my embrace,
In your arms, I've found my sacred place.
With you, I'm whole, forever complete,
Our love story, my dear, is oh so sweet.

"Embracing Eternity:
A Love Unfurled"

In the stillness of night, I yearned and sighed,
For the dawn to break, my heart open wide,
Crossing roads and farms, a hundred mile,
My soul ablaze, fueled by love's tender smile.

To embrace her form, my fervent desire,
In those tender arms, I'd never tire,
She, my love's cornerstone, heart's abode,
In her eyes, my world's vibrant odes.

Oh, the girl so dear, my heart's pure song,
Her laughter, a melody, all day long,
Her tears, a storm I wish to dispel,
In her embrace, all doubts and fears quell.

Whispers of her hair, a fragrant breeze,
Enveloping warmth, putting my heart at ease,
In her presence, life finds its tether,
In her love's embrace, I'd roam forever.

For that radiant smile, my soul does pine,
In her loving arms, a lifeline divine,
Day and night, the embrace I crave,
In her love's haven, my heart finds its wave.
Its her whom i want to submerge myself deep,
In my arms its her whom i want to forever keep.

"Eternal Hope:
Love's flower Unfolds"

In the realm of dreams, my heart finds its tether,
A hope sprouts strong, to bind us together,
To make you mine, in this endless endeavor,
To cherish your laughter, to hold you forever.

I yearn for the day, to make you my own,
To embrace your soul, to be fully known,
In the gentle whispers of twilight's tone,
We'll dance in love, in a world we've sown.

Every smile you wear, a constellation bright,
Illuminating my nights, dispelling the night,
In your tender gaze, there's a pure moonlight,
A promise of love, burning ever so bright.

Kisses planted gently on your silken skin,
A tapestry woven, where our love begins,
Each touch, each caress, a love-filled hymn,
In this symphony of us, our hearts will spin.

Forever entwined, like vines on a vineyard's tree,
In the tapestry of love, we'll write our decree,
Hand in hand, facing life's vast, wild sea,
Our hope unbreakable, a timeless esprit.

With you, my love, every moment's a treasure,
A hope to be yours, it's a love without measure,
To hold you close, to find joy beyond measure,
My hope to make you mine, an eternal, radiant pleasure.

"Eternal Embrace:
Love Beyond the Skies"

In the realm of days adorned with glee,
Her gift of joy flows abundantly.
In tender embrace, my heart she cheers,
Drowning my fears, calming my fears.

Oh, if this grip could last beyond the skies,
Where eternity dances, where love never dies,
I wish their trust in my love would be,
An unbroken bond, for all to see.

Wrapped in my arms, worries dissolve and fade,
Like a gentle stream through a tranquil glade.
No hesitations in love's warm embrace,
Only love that time cannot erase.

Eternal flames of love, we shall tend,
A love that lasts, with no final end.
Till the stars lose their shimmering light,
I'll hold them close, every day and every night.

For love knows no bounds, no earthly tether,
It stretches far and wide, beyond measure.
I wish to hold them, a love so true,
Till eternity and beyond, just us two.

"Whispers of Maybe:
Love's Eternal Promise"

In the realm of promises, I took my stand,
With every solemn vow, I held her hand,
"No touch," I pledged, to keep a distant shore,
"No closeness," whispered, my heart feeling sore.

"No kiss," I promised, as time did unwind,
"No hopes," I promised, aching in my mind,
Each oath, a layer, peeled from my loving heart,
Yet, love remained, refusing to depart.

She's my home, a smile upon my soul,
Yet life stole happiness, exacting its toll,
In draining thoughts, etched on memory's stone,
A flicker of "maybe," in whispers, it's sown.

Dreams of being 'Us,' in reality's embrace,
Longing to hold her, in love's tender grace,
Yet this reality remains a distant glimmer,
A hope that burns, heart's eternal simmer.

Each day I survive, clinging to that hope,
In whispers of "maybe," my heart finds scope,
Till the final breath, I'll carry this desire,
That she'll confess love & set my soul on fire.

In my last sigh, may her name take a flight,
In the gentle breeze, carrying my love's light,
For in this world, we were a "maybe" cast,
But in the next, a reality to hold steadfast.

In a future reborn, destiny to unfurl,
A truth unchained, our love will swirl,
In that life a new promise, true and free,
Forever entwined, just her and me.

"Boundless Embrace:
A Love Beyond Time"

In the realm where rules dared to break,
I held her close, a bold move to make,
A tight embrace, a kiss so light,
As stars bore witness to our heartfelt night.

Her essence submerged within my arms,
A completeness, casting away all harms,
Soft touch melded, a fusion divine,
A whispering promise: "forever, you're mine."

Her gaze radiant, face warm and aglow,
A connection so strong, a love to grow,
I wished that moment would never depart,
Forever she'd stay, melded to my heart.

Boundaries shattered for love's sweet bloom,
In that night's embrace, chased away the gloom,
No doubts lingered in love's tender air,
A masterpiece painted, beyond compare.

Expressing care, affection, pure delight,
In the canopy of stars, our love took flight,
For us, a desire to be entwined,
Leaving worries and fears far behind.

In the vast expanse of time and space,
I yearn to hold her in a love's embrace,
For my love runs deep, untainted, and pure,
Endless and strong, forever to endure.

This heart longs for her, each passing day,
Craving her hug, her smile's gentle sway,
Her happiness, her warmth, her tender hold,
In the symphony of love, the tale is told.

"I love you till the end of time," I avow,
In every beat, in each breath, in then and now,
A love that transcends the ticking of the clock,
In eternity's embrace, forever we dock.

"Whispers of Devotion:
A Dance Through Shadows"

In shadows cast by love's soft light,
My heart's truth whispers through the night,
For there are moments, bittersweet,
When distance makes our hearts compete.

I ache when you pull away,
Hurted, wounded, lost in dismay,
Longing to hold your tender hand,
Yet understanding, I withstand.

For I cherish your happiness,
More than my own heart's distress,
In the dance of love's refrain,
I endure the echoes of pain.

I live with the truth in my chest,
That your comfort is my quest,
To keep you smiling, my delight,
Even if it dims my own light.

Yet, deep within, my love stays,
Unwavering through nights and days,
A devotion that forever speaks,
Of love that's strong, love that seeks.

My heart beats solely for you,
A love that's pure, a love that's true,
Each beat a promise, each pulse a rhyme,
In sync with yours, through endless time.

I care for you, my soul, my dear,
A love that's beyond all fear,
And every day that we're apart,
I hold you close within my heart.

Dreaming of the day you'll see,
This love that binds both you and me,
Smiling, you'll come to my embrace,
Infinite love, our eternal grace.

We'll promise to make this love our own,
A love that's steadfast, fully grown,
Cherishing our bond through the years,
With endless love, conquering all fears..

"Eternal Embrace:
A Symphony of Pink Hues"

In her attire adorned with hues of pink,
There she strolls, my heart's link,
Those long hairs framing her tender face,
The only vision I crave to chase.

Her beauty, a force that drew my fall,
Cuteness that enchants with a gentle call,
In every step, a magnetic grace,
This girl I love, my destined embrace.

I long to journey life by her side,
In her care, my fears shall subside,
Her smile, worth a hundred miles,
In her love is where my heart compiles.

A forehead yearning for a tender kiss,
In her presence, all worries I dismiss,
Her hand, I wish to clasp so tight,
Walking together in love's tender light.

Every breath whispers prayers for her joy,
For her success, my hopes deploy,
I run to keep her safe and warm,
Close to her, my soul finds its norm.

In silent love, my heart finds its voice,
A love eternal, a timeless choice,
Till my last breath, this love shall stay,
Guiding her through life's every way.

When my time comes to bid goodbye,
I'll be a star in the vast sky,
Granting wishes, her desires I'll fulfill,
In her heart, my love will echo still.

For she completes my being's chart,
In her gaze, I find my start,
Her smile ignites my joyous flame,
In her love, I find my forever claim.

Through ages past, my love's decree,
To spend my life, eternally free,
With her, my heart shall ever soar,
In love's embrace, forevermore.

"Nocturnal Embrace:
A Love Unfading"

In the depths of night, memories reside,
A love so pure, our hearts did confide.
Last night's embrace, forever a part,
Soul's entwined, never to depart.

Our skins in harmony, a tender ballet,
Whispers of love in the moonlight's array.
Kisses planted on cheeks so fair,
And necks where passion danced in the air.

Your grasp, fierce and full of fire,
Ignited a blaze, a deep, burning desire.
Touches etched in time's tender hold,
Infinite love stories, forever to be told.

Divine emotions, an unearthly hue,
Truth in every word, every breath I drew.
Wishing that night would never find its end,
Craving for you, my eternal friend.

Hands ache for your gentle trace,
Yearning for the warmth of your embrace.
Thirsting for your essence, fervent and true,
Longing for a love renewed, just me and you.

Until we meet again, the ache will stay,
Love transcending boundaries, come what may.
Forever I'll cherish, without a mime,
You're my endless love, till the end of time.

"Infinite Love:
A Symphony Unspoken"

In a world where words strain to portray,
The depth of love that words can't convey,
She asked, "Why do you love me so?"
A question that set my heart aglow.

Through countless seasons, I've patiently waited,
For your love, my soul unabated,
Your smile, a beacon of my delight,
Guiding me through the darkest night.

In your tender touch, my heart finds home,
A desire to never again roam,
An ardent love that's stood the test,
Now yearns to cradle you to rest.

Your elegance, a magnetic grace,
Your charm, a spell I can't erase,
In the language of your eyes, I find,
A narrative of love, pure and kind.

Since the days of friendship and old,
Our love has blossomed, strong and bold,
Through midnight texts and songs we sung,
My love for you, a song forever young.

Through years gone by, my love persisted,
In every memory, it's insisted,
It lives in the present, vibrant and true,
And with each day, it only grew.

How do I express your profound worth?
In your joy, I find my own mirth,
Your tears, a pain that cuts so deep,
Your smile, a secret I long to keep.

In your embrace, I find my might,
Your touch, a flame that feels just right,
The way you gaze, my heart takes flight,
A symphony of love, both soft and bright.

My soul yearns to serve you, to care,
My body longs to forever share,
The cute allure that pulls me near,
Your lips, a destination so clear.

Your waist, a grasp I ache to hold,
In tender hours, our love unfolds,
Conversations endless, sweet and deep,
A love so vast, forever to keep.

Infinite love, a boundless sea,
Yet inadequate, words fail me,
With all my heart and all my soul,
My love for you, an eternal whole.

"Unseen Love:
A Diamond in the Night"

In the deep abyss of night, stars alight, I ponder and I pine,
Thoughts of you dance in my mind, a love that's so divine.
Yet, you remain afar, unaware of this heart's tender chime,
A love unperceived, like a hidden gem through time.

My affection, like a diamond, crafted within my soul's embrace,
Each facet polished with devotion, every corner, every grace,
Delicate as rain's first drop, on a leaf, it finds its place,
Yet, you remain oblivious, lost in life's hurried race.

I've poured my essence into you, a sacrifice so true,
Emptying my being, every ounce, my love imbued in you,
In your presence, I've found my abode, my peace so new,
In the cradle of your arms, I wish to dream and pursue.

Decades have adorned my love, each day a growing vine,
Watered with your smiles, nurtured by the joy you consign,
In the soil of my care, it blooms, an eternally tender sign,
A flower of love, longing to be yours, forever thine.

This bloom desires to dwell, embraced within your chest,
As the sky, the sun, the moon, and stars bear witness to my quest,
May the truth of my love someday in your heart manifest,
As I patiently wait for that moment, in hope, I'm blessed.

"Endless Rhyme:
A Love Beyond Time"

In a world where hearts often stray,
Yours, a beacon, lights my way,
No one's touched my soul like you,
A love so pure, forever true.

In the depths of time's relentless flow,
Your love awakened a part I'd yet to know,
A melody sweet, my heart it played,
And now for you, it beats, unswayed.

No horizon can break this bond so tight,
It's you I'll cherish, morning to night,
In your embrace, my universe finds its rhyme,
Forever and beyond, till the end of time.

Your smile, a sun that warms my days,
In your love, my heart forever stays,
Every moment spent in your grace,
A testament to love's enduring embrace.

Like a gentle breeze on a summer's day,
Your presence soothes, keeps troubles at bay,
In your eyes, I see my destiny,
A love so deep, it sets my spirit free.

Through life's highs and lows, we'll stride,
In your love, I'll always confide,
You've etched your name upon my soul,
In love's symphony, you're the sacred scroll.

No force can break what we've become,
A love so true, it makes my heart strum,
Till the stars dim and the sun no longer gleams,
I'll hold you close, and share our dreams.

Time may dance, and seasons wane,
But our love shall remain, a sweet refrain,
For you've imprinted on my very core,
A love everlasting, forevermore.

In the tapestry of fate, we're intertwined,
In the book of love, our story's signed,
Forever I'll love you, beyond this rhyme,
Till the end of time, you'll forever be mine.

"Hearts in Eternity:
A Tale of Transient Glory"

In the vast tapestry of fate, we were delayed,
Our paths diverged, destiny played its charade,
Why did we suffer in solitude's ember,
Before we found our hearts' tender November?

Completeness found in your soul's embrace,
A union of love, a sacred space,
Yet, were we truly incomplete before?
Or did we yearn for something more?

O beauty with an ebony hue,
In this tangled dance, we both withdrew,
Love's torment, a bitter brew,
Yet, through it all, my heart stayed true.

Countless hours in contemplation,
Navigating love's vast formation,
As if a debt to life I owed,
In your presence, my spirit glowed.

O cherished one, you set me free,
A voyager in the night, destiny's decree,
Morning came, bidding a reluctant adieu,
But my love for you, forever true.

While life's breath was still within,
I couldn't claim your heart and win,
In the throes of death, I confess,
Paying love's due, my heart's redress.

In the echoes of our untold story,
Lies the essence of our transient glory,
Through time and space, our love transcends,
A tale of hearts, where eternity mends.

"Melodies of the Heart:
A Ballad in Echoes of Love"

In the silent realms of my beating heart,
You're the serenade, the timeless art.
Whispers soft, like a gentle breeze,
Carry the echoes of love that never cease.

In the ballad of unfulfilled dreams we share,
You're the confidant, always there.
Your presence, a beacon in shadows deep,
A secret keeper, my heart's promise to keep.

Through tempests that rage and calms so serene,
Your memory paints a vivid, lingering scene.
A portrait framed in the gallery of my mind,
In the tapestry of time, your essence entwined.

Stormy nights may veil the moon's soft glow,
Yet, your love's radiance continues to grow.
In the sunlit days and the twilight's grace,
You're the anchor, the steady embrace.

In the melody of sorrows, in laughter's embrace,
You're the solace, the smile on my face.
A healing touch, a comforting sight,
In the darkest hour, you're my guiding light.

The book of my life, a tale yet untold,
In its pages, your story unfolds.
But your absence, a poignant refrain,
Leaves a silence, a melancholic strain.

Oh, my love, my soul's eternal rhyme,
In the chapters of time, you stand sublime.
As the symphony of life plays its song,
You're the harmony that keeps me strong.

Through the ebb and flow, the joy and strife,
You're the thread that weaves my life.
In the canvas of existence, you're the theme,
A recurring note in the love's grand scheme.

So, in the shadows where emotions start,
You're the melody of my confiding heart.
Whispers echo softly, dispelling fear,
In the ballad of love, you're always near.

"Whispers of Love:
Navigating the Winds of Fate"

In a realm where faith is strong and fair,
I'll place you, a jewel, beyond compare.
If not yours, I'll be none other's part,
Bound by a love that's a work of art.

The winds whisk secrets, where do they steer?
Guiding us both, a path unclear.
Rebellious gusts, how they play and tease,
Leading you, me, where the future sees.

Yet the winds, elusive, don't unveil their quest,
We sail together, in a hopeful jest.
How long will your memories gently tether?
Through seasons passing, memories gather.

Morning light and dusk's embrace,
Carry echoes of your gentle grace.
In the city of thoughts, you're the gleaming tower,
Winds chant your name, an empowering bower.

Mysterious whispers, what do they convey,
As the winds beckon on this winding way?
In this enigma, where fate's compass wanes,
We navigate the unknown terrains.

Your face, a mirage in dreams so deep,
A secret's keep that my heart shall keep.
You're my present, my love's true hue,
In devotion, my heart's compass points to you.

In the tapestry of time, woven rare and bright,
In the whispers of stars that guide the night,
In the cradle of dreams where memories reside,
In the symphony of life, you forever preside.

A chapter may close, but love's tale remains,
In my heart's gallery, you're the masterpiece that reigns.
In the canvas of destiny, strokes of love persist,
A love unbound, timeless and existent.

Though parted by distance, we're bound by soul's song,
In the lyrics of love, you still belong.
In the pulse of every heartbeat, you gently reside,
My love, forever with you, our love will abide.

All prayers ascend, adorned with your name,
In the temple of love, you're the eternal flame.

"Whispers of Time:
Love's Uncharted Journey"

In the depths of my heart, a love profound,
For you, my dear, the sweetest I've found,
Your eyes, a universe, they silently speak,
Their beauty captivating, making my soul peak.

A smile upon your lips, a strike of light,
It brightens my days, oh what a sight,
It makes my face glow with an inner cheer,
Your smile, my love, so genuine and dear.

The touch of your hand, a gentle embrace,
A fleeting moment, a tender grace,
I yearn for it, a craving forever,
An incomplete wish, I endeavor.

But the sands of time slip through my grasp,
As uncertainty weaves this enigmatic clasp,
You hold back, unsure of my love's embrace,
Leaving my heart in a bittersweet space.

Yet your happiness is my utmost desire,
In the warmth of joy, I shall never tire,
To see you safe, surrounded by glee,
Is all my affection wishes it to be.

In another life, perhaps we'll align,
At the right time, our stars entwine,
In the perfect place, love shall bloom,
And your heart for me, then will resume.

Till that destined day, I'll cherish each morn,
In the echoes of memories, love reborn,
With each passing day, my love will grow,
For you, my darling, I'll eternally show.

Maybe fate has a plan, a path to carve,
A journey of love, where our hearts will starve,
Yet hope persists, in the next life we might find,
A love so true, forever entwined.

Till then, my love, from afar I'll be,
Loving you dearly, till eternity,
In the whispers of time, I'll softly pine,
For you, my love, i will forever love,
till the end of the time...

"Eternal Patience:
*A Love That Transcends Time**

In the realm of timeless echoes, once again I fall,
Memories surging, a familiar beckoning call.
Though paths have shifted, we still stride side by side,
Sometimes changed, yet the essence can't hide.

Eyes locked upon you, as in days of core,
Beauty untarnished, my heart you restore.
Completing me, a wish unfulfilled but true,
In every heartbeat, my love for you has always grew.

Your smile, a canvas of the past's gentle art,
A laughter, a melody that captured my heart.
In quiet steps, I've followed you unseen,
Silent witness to your joys and dreams.

I bear your pain, a burden shared in kind,
To ease your sorrows, a mission of love defined.
Knowing love's journey may not lead to my embrace,
Yet, my devotion for you shall never lose its grace.

In this ephemeral dance, my hope remains,
In the silhouette of time, where destiny ordains.
Though I can't dwell in your tender embrace,
Having you near is my solace, my saving grace.

In another life, I dream we'll be entwined,
Two souls converging, destiny realigned.
Until that dawn, I'll cherish what we share,
Endless devotion and love beyond compare.

With patience and hope, my heart remains aglow,
In this love, eternal, I'll wait, I'll wait, I'll grow.

"Serenade of a Silent Love:
Waiting Until the End of Time"

And one more night i slept in pain
Keeping my head against the window pane
That resistance was all that offered
That pushing away was all that expected
The love which was again in the boundaries set,
Like a beautiful pigeon torchered in the net,
That love which also wanted to fly in sky
But within the blames it only had to stood in why
Why for answering the worth and sigh
Cant tell the truth and have to say the lie,
Lie by ignoring the question or answering something other
As if " no" is the predefined decision, then why to bother ?
Why to describe the love in words, when its a feeling to feel
It's her, i want to propose while holding her hand & doing the kneel
Its her whom i want to hug till my last breath,
Its her whom i want to kiss in her every skin,
In a way that she forgets all the pain in past she's been
Smooching her lips,i want to tell her all,
All the secrets, like the stars from the sky so fall,

Placing my kisses in abundance on her neck
Creases shouldn't be there on her forehead is to check
As the crease on the lips is important then the forehead,
Untill i surpass from this world, will love till my last breath..
And will wait that she kisses me back with all her love sometime,
I will wait for her,untill then ,till the end of time...

"Bound by Love,
A Prayer for Tomorrow"

Painfull it is to survive each day,
With you so close, yet so far
Like a diamond yet so star,
Away from me you will leave me some day,
Still coming to you every other day,
To complete "us" in a way,
That you miss "us" even being far away,
And yes am deprive from your love,
As you have stated boundaries for "us"
These boundaries which have winded my heart,
In a way like a cactus pricking the flower,
And the blood which is dripping down from my heart,
Still yet craves for your love, to give it a start,
The drips of blood which are flowing down to the floor,
Still takes your name with love, deep from the core
And every now and then when you will fall in path,
You will find me by your side, standing like a guard,
Keeping you warm, and keeping you safe,
Forever you are my love and by having you in arms,
I will win this world, with every bit of charm,

Every day doing the hustle,i only pray for the dawn,
As it is when i meet you, walking down the lawn,
May you realise my love so deep,
Forever you want my heart, with you to keep,
As i have given myself all into you,
Now i havent left my anything with me,
Its all you who i am, and its you all whom i live,
And in this way,i love you each day,
No matter where tomorrow, how far you stay..

"Heart's Ballet:
Longing in Silence"

Enduring the ache with each passing day,
Near yet distant, you hold sway,
A gem but distant like a star's array,
Someday you'll part, a price to pay,
Still, I come to bridge our own display,
Completing "us" in a unique ballet,
Longing for "us" even when you're far away,
Boundaries set, love held at bay,
A cactus pricks, love in disarray,
Yet, my heart yearns for a fresh start,
Blood drips, love from my core, a tender art,
Whispers your name as it hits the floor,
In every beat, your love I implore,
By your side, I'll stand so sure,
In your warmth, my love will endure,
You're my forever, my love, my allure,
In your embrace, I conquer, love so pure,
Through the toil, I await the morn,
When on the lawn, our love is reborn,
Hoping you fathom my love's deep thorn,

Yearning to keep my heart in your bourn,
For I've given all, in love I've sworn,
In this devotion, each day I'm drawn,
No matter where you dwell at dawn.

"Mirror of Love:
Fragrance Through Time"

In a realm where truth's unveiled through glass,
The mirror holds secrets, memories amassed,
Of hugs so tight, of closeness sweet,
Our souls entwined, a love complete.

Submerged in arms, a symphony so grand,
Our intimacy fused, hand in hand,
Like rivers merging into the boundless sea,
Our souls as one, forever to be.

I yearn to blend my body's tender trace,
With yours, in a dance of timeless grace,
Let my soul's aroma embrace your soul,
A fragrant tale, our love's eternal scroll.

Let our scents linger, an everlasting rhyme,
Beyond fleeting days, transcending time,
So even when fate parts our tender ways,
Our souls entwined, in love's eternal blaze.

For when distance dares to pull us apart,
Our hearts shall beat as one, a timeless art,
Invisible threads of love, they'll weave,
Each passing moment, a love to believe.

Through the whispers of the wind, we'll hear,
Each other's laughter, each other's tear,
In the embrace of night, we'll reunite,
Our love's eternal flame, forever bright.

Though miles may lay a vast divide,
Our love shall conquer, hearts open wide,
For in the mirror of love, we find,
A love unbound, a love entwined.

And the mirror knows all the truths we share,
Of love so pure, beyond compare,
In its reflection, our love shall gleam,
A timeless love, an everlasting dream.

"Echoes of Eternity:
Love's echo Unveiled".

In the dance of shadows, where our love began,
A tapestry of moments, woven strand by strand.
The mirror reflects our laughter, our tears,
Capturing the symphony of our fleeting years.

In the soft echo of whispers, secrets untold,
A story of passion, in the verses we hold.
Our silhouettes entwined, a celestial rhyme,
A serenade of hearts, beating in perfect time.

And the mirror knows all the truths,
Of all the hugs, of all the closeness,
Of all that intimacy within which we indulged,
In each other's arms, our souls fully bulged.

I want to rub my body with yours in such a way,
That my scent lingers, an essence to stay.
The fragrance of my soul, a delicate perfume,
A lingering presence, filling every room.

And so does yours with me, an exchange divine,
A mingling of spirits, an eternal sign.
Maybe this way, even if we part someday,
Our souls connected, in an unbroken array.

For love transcends the boundaries of time,
In the verses of our hearts, an endless rhyme.
The echoes of our laughter, the warmth we share,
A timeless connection, beyond compare.

In the tapestry of moments, woven with grace,
Our love story echoes in every embrace.
As the sun sets on the canvas of our prime,
Our love will endure till the end of time.

"Whispers of Eternal Love:
A Tale Unveiled"

In the realm of unforeseen fate, it came to be,
A tale of love, vast and free, between you and me.
Silent whispers marked the finish line of my days,
Departing without goodbyes, in enigmatic ways.

As air, I'll pass through the worldly stream,
Is love truly as fair as it may seem?
Days fleeting by, each a shattering glass,
In your acceptance, a question did amass.

Could you not embrace me in your tender grace,
As nature shifts through this temporal space?
Yet, for your happiness, I pledge my heart's affection,
A love eternal, beyond life's earthly direction.

In the hours unseen, love blossomed with might,
A beacon in darkness, guiding through night.
Even if fate weaves a different end to our tale,
My love for you shall prevail, steadfast and hale.

For your smile, I'd paint the skies a hue so blue,
Yet, in your silence, a question forever grew.
But my love will endure, timeless and true,
A vow whispered to the stars, just for you.

Through the ebbs and flows of life's swift stream,
In the silence of night, and the light of dream,
I'll be there, a love that remains unwavering,
A melody of the heart, always persevering.

In the corridors of time, our love shall find its way,
Unspoken, unbroken, forever it'll sway.
As the sun sets and the moon takes its climb,
My love for you endures, till the end of time.

"Shadows of Love:
Yearning for Forever"

In the shadows of night, I longed to remain,
Embracing you close, through joy and pain,
Craving the warmth of your tender bond,
In the whispers of love, our souls respond.

Aching to taste your lips, a soft, sweet song,
Our hearts entwined, a love lifelong,
To feel your being melded with my own,
Completing the puzzle, in love we've known.

Seeking to hold you, secure and tight,
Assuring love's endurance, through darkest night,
Whispering vows into the moon's soft light,
Easing your fears, making all things right.

Every inch of you, a sacred, cherished part,
Yearning to explore, soul-to-soul, heart-to-heart,
Hours fleeting like seconds, in love's sweetest art,
In this timeless bond, we'll never drift apart.

Clutching your hand, steadfast and true,
Showing my love in deeds old and new,
For you are my world, my guiding light,
In your presence, everything feels just right.

Yet, a struggle lingers to make you perceive,
The depth of my love, how it continues to heave,
Each day, my feelings grow, sincere and deep,
A love profound, secrets our hearts keep.

In your absence, I ache, I pine, I miss,
Each touch, each stolen, tender kiss,
Yearning for the moment you understand,
That my love for you forever takes a stand.

Prayers woven with love, gentle and grace,
Holding your essence, in this warm embrace,
Hoping that time will gently unfurl,
The love I hold, for you,
As you are my only world.

"Decade of Devotion:
Love's Timeless Journey"

For a decade, my heart's been bound,
In love with you, a treasure found.
Till my last breath, this love shall last,
Through future's trials, present, and past.

Cherished moments, our times together,
In my heart, they'll stay, now and forever.
I'll chase away your worries, keep you light,
To see your smile, my endless delight.

Through lows and highs, I'll by your side,
No other support could ever provide.
I'll be your rock, your shelter, your guide,
In every storm, in every stride.

Our hugs, our touches, I'll always miss,
Each moment spent, a stolen kiss.
But the dread of losing you, my dear,
Wakes me up in terror, fills me with fear.

In dreams, I lose you, day by day,
It's a nightmare I wish would fade away.
To wake without you, my heart can't bear,
The thought of a world without you there.

So, I'll hold you close, never let you go,
Travel miles to be with you, it's a must, I know.
To keep you near, my one desire,
To quell the flames of that fearful fire.

In your presence, my dreams come true,
A reality so sweet, a love so true.
I can't imagine a life without your grace,
In your love, I've found my special place.

With you, my love, it's forever to be,
A journey of love, just you and me.
Till my last breath, you're the one I'll adore,
In your love, I'll cherish forevermore.

"Endless Apology:
Love's Redemption Song"

In the depths of my heart, I admit my wrongs,
I've caused you pain with careless words and songs.
I made you cry, in the autumn's early light,
Your teardrops fell like dew in the silent night.

Leaning on the wall, you wept so deep,
I promise, your tears, in my memory, I'll keep.
Guilt courses through my veins, I know I was blind,
But you, my soulmate, you're the one I'll find.

I can't bear to live without your loving grace,
You're my only need, in this vast, empty space.
I'm sorry for the hurt, the tears I've made you cry,
I'll cherish you forever, till the day I die.

I yearn for our hugs, for our sweet talks so true,
The way you said my name, how I miss that too.
Your touch, your smile, your laughter's gentle chime,
I miss "us" deeply, till the end of time.

In your love, I'll remain, forever by your side,
My heart, my soul, with you, forever shall abide.
I promise to care, to pray, to hold you tight,
As i will forever love you endlessly,
Day and night....

"Unyielding Love:
A Promise Beyond Time"

In the realm of love, my heart's aglow,
For a girl, it's you, I truly know.
And the day you believe my love, just let me know,
I've given myself, there's nothing more to bestow.

Each day, my thoughts, they turn to you,
Your smile, your laughter, like morning's dew.
You are the one my heart beats for, it's true,
My love for you, forever strong and true.

I trust your words, I trust your grace,
In your actions, I find my happy place.
This love I hold, in its purest embrace,
I've surrendered myself, in every case.

I trust you more than I trust my own way,
In your presence, my doubts, they fade away.
You know my flaws, my foolish display,
But this love, unyielding, is here to stay.

I may be naive, I may be a child,
But my love for you, it's undefiled.
Though you may seek someone more mild,
My heart's forever yours, reconciled.

As time marches on, this love won't decay,
It will shine like gold, come what may.
In every moment, in every way,
I'll care for you, love you, day by day.

I'll wait for you, in the moon's soft glow,
Till my last breath, this you must know.
My heart is yours, no matter where you go,
In your love, I'll eternally bask and grow.

So, take your time, find your own way,
For I'll be here, come what may.
This love, unwavering, is here to stay,
In your arms, I'll forever lay.

"Love's Silent Vigil:
A Decade of Waiting"

In the realm of love, I find my fate,
With all the passion, I'll patiently wait,
For the girl I adore, in my heart's embrace,
I'll hold my love, in this sacred space.

Though you may depart, seek another's hand,
I'll stand steadfast, on love's golden strand,
I'll wait through the seasons, through joy and strife,
Cherishing memories, the moments of life.

A decade's connection, so deep and true,
Our hearts entwined, as the years swiftly flew,
But love unspoken, a silent affection,
Held in my heart, with unwavering devotion.

I'll keep these emotions, my secret, my muse,
In the depths of my soul, where my love I'll infuse,
For your radiant smile, and those tender hugs,
I'll wait with a heart that's bound by love's lugs.

The moments we've shared, the laughter and tears,
Have etched their marks throughout the years,
Every glance, every word, every unspoken desire,
Ignites the flames of love, a passionate fire.

I'll wait for the day you discover this truth,
The love that's been hidden, the eternal proof,
When you find your way back into my arms,
I'll cherish the moment, with all of love's charms.

Through the trials and tests, through the darkest of days,
I'll wait for the time our love finds its ways,
In patience, I'll linger, in hope, I'll abide,
With love as my beacon, in you, I confide.

So, as time marches on, and life takes its course,
I'll carry this love, with unwavering force,
For the girl whom I cherish, my heart's sweetest fate,
In silence and patience, I'll wait, I'll wait.

"Echoes of Love:
Two Weeks After"

Two weeks after, I saw her grace,
A fleeting smile, a glimpse of her face.

Her smile, like a sunbeam, so briefly shone,
Yet it lit up my world, my heart was overthrown.
For in those seconds, I found my delight,
Knowing my words, my humour, brought forth the light.

Two weeks after, we walked side by side,
My heart danced with joy, I couldn't hide.
To share that space, to feel her near,
Brought happiness that banished all fear.

Two weeks after, she spoke to me,
Although not for long but we conversed, my heart full of glee.
Her voice, a melody, a soothing song,
I knew in my heart, she truly belonged.

It's her happiness, her laughter so pure,
That I cherish, that I'll forever endure.
Her smile, a treasure, so gentle and warm,
In the depths of my soul, it will always transform.

She is the one I long for, in silence I adore,
A love so profound, it grows more and more.
In this life, I'll wait, though my love's concealed,
For she's the one whose presence I'll never yield.

Till the day I depart from this world of mine,
My heart will hold onto this love so divine.
And in the next life, I'll seek her once more,
For she's my favorite wish, incomplete, yet pure.

So my heart and my soul, they'll patiently wait,
For the love that's destined, for this beautiful fate.
Till the end of time, my love will endure,
For she's the one I'll forever and truly adore.

"Whispers of Forever:
A Love Beyond Time"

In the distance, I watch you shine like a star,
Your happiness and smiles, seen from afar.
As long as you're cheering, my heart's at ease,
My love for you, a gentle, timeless breeze.

In the chamber of memories, our moments reside,
The dances, the laughter, side by side.
I'll treasure them always, a love so pure,
In the tapestry of our past, they endure.

Whenever you tremble, when fear draws near,
I'll be your solace, wiping every tear.
May blessings rain down upon you, my dear,
Success and happiness, year after year.

I'll fade like the smoke in the dusk's embrace,
Lost in the mist, leaving no trace.
But your name I'll carry, a whispered refrain,
Cherishing our love, in joy or in pain.

In the sands of time, I'll find my reprieve,
With each grain, in memories, I'll weave.
Searching in the next life for a love so true,
Hoping to find a girl just like you.

Though I'll be gone, in this life we part,
You'll always own a piece of my heart.
In love's eternal dance, we'll meet again like a trend,
Forever and after, my dearest lovely friend.

"Dreams Unveiled:
In the Silence of Night"

In the hush of night, I saw her there,
Sleeping like a child, so sweet and fair,
The girl whom I love, my dream come true,
With every breath, my heart she'd subdue.

Her touch, a spark, ignites a fiery start,
Through veins, like lightning, it courses my heart,
When I hold her hand, I'm on top of the world,
For in her embrace, my joy is unfurled.

Her gaze, a spell, draws me ever near,
In her eyes, there's nothing to fear,
Her beauty, a beacon in the darkest night,
Guiding my soul with its gentle light.

I know my love may be an unfulfilled wish,
But when she's close, I find my life's bliss,
Complete in her presence, my heart's delight,
Forever by her side, through day and night.

Though my love may remain an incomplete dream,
In her arms, life's a vibrant, flowing stream,
I'll cherish her always, my love so pure,
With each passing moment, my devotion is sure.

I'll strive to keep her happiness aglow,
Till the end of time, my love will only grow,
For the girl I adore, my heart's true friend,
With her, my love story shall never end.

"Endless Embrace:
A Love That Transcends Time"

In the depths of my heart, you'll always reside,
A love so profound, in which I take pride.
I yearn to hold your hand, feel your embrace,
To kiss your lips, in this endless chase.

With warmth that's undying, our souls entwined,
In your arms, I long to be, so kind.
To feel you closely, your essence so sweet,
Our love's a fire that'll never face defeat.

I cherish the memories we've shared, my dear,
The hugs, the talks, the laughter so clear.
Our closeness, a bond that time can't erase,
Your smile, your eyes, and your skin's gentle grace.

Each moment etched in my heart's deepest rhyme,
I'll love you always till the end of time.
This love, a flame that'll forever burn bright,
Guiding me through the darkest of night.

Though we may be apart, in different places,
Our love's the thread that time never erases.
As the stars above in the vast, endless sky,
Our love will endure, and never say goodbye.

In my heart, you'll forever have a place,
A love so pure, a never-ending embrace.
For you are the one, my heart's sweetest chime,
I'll love you endlessly till the end of time.

"Birthday Wishes:
Love's Eternal Celebration"

Happy Birthday to the girl I adore,
Whose smile lights up my world, that's for sure.
May God fulfill your wishes, every one,
May you succeed, your journey just begun.

I promise, always, by your side I'll be,
Supporting, guiding, just you wait and see.
On this special day, your joy is the key,
To unlock a future as bright as can be.

Keep smiling, my love, with that radiant grace,
In your parents' eyes, you're a shining embrace.
I'll stand beside you through every climb,
For you, my dear, until the end of time.

Your laughter, a melody, a song so sweet,
As we dance through life, our hearts will beat.
So blow out those candles, make a wish anew,
I'll be your constant, forever and true.

Happy Birthday to you, my dearest friend,
May this day's joy on your path descend.
With love and warmth, our hearts entwine,
Forever yours, in your life's design.

As the years go by, and the seasons flow,
In the garden of life, our love will grow.
Happy Birthday to you, the one I hold dear,
Your happiness, my love, is my greatest cheer.

So on this day, as we celebrate you,
Know that my love is steadfast and true.
In your smile, in your laughter, in every embrace,
I find my refuge, my happy place.

May your dreams soar high, may your heart find peace,
With each passing day, our love won't cease.
Happy Birthday, my love, my eternal rhyme,
I'll be there for you, throughout
Till the end of time.

"Enduring Echoes:
A Love Beyond Time"

The only smile i was staring on,
The only face which glows my face
The one whose birthday was like a festive for me
All went well,as she smiled
All was worth as happiness gave the approval
And as long as she is happy,
As long as she is smiling,
My every ounce of energy and run is of worth
As she is the one whom I crave for ,
She is the one whom i love
And forever i will continue to love her,
As she matters to me till deep in my heart
Through the echoes of time, my pledge to endure,
A love so steadfast, unbreakable and pure.
Till the end of days, till the final chime,
She matters to me, beyond the bounds of time.
In the tapestry of our love, woven with care,
Her smile, a gem, beyond compare.
And as the stars witness our eternal rhyme,
I'll love her till the end, throughout all time

"Eternal Smiles:
A Love that Transcends Time"

In your smile, a world did I behold,
A face that made my heart's desires unfold.
Your birthday, like a grand and joyous fete,
For me, my love, no day could ever beat.

Your smile, a treasure, brighter than the sun,
In its warmth, my heart had finally won.
Happiness, the seal of your sweet approval,
For you, my love, I'd scale the highest spire.

As long as you're happy, my heart's delight,
I'd chase the stars, reach for the highest height.
Every ounce of energy, every stride,
Dedicated to you, forever by your side.

My love for you, a craving, deep and true,
In the darkest night, in the morning's dew.
Forever, this love in my heart shall bloom,
For you, my darling, I'd chase the moon.

Till the end of time, till the very last breath,
I'll cherish you, my love, beyond life and death.
In your embrace, my soul finds its abode,
You're the one I love, on this sacred road.

So, let the world turn, the seasons pass by,
With you, my love, I'll reach for the sky.
In your smile, my purpose and my worth,
Forever and always, until the end of the earth.

In your laughter, my heart finds its tune,
Underneath the silver of the crescent moon.
You're the one I adore, you're the one I hold dear,
In your love, forever, I'll be near.

With you, my love, I've found my home,
In your eyes, the place where I'll always roam.
Till the end of time, till the final rhyme,
You're the one I love, for all of time.
Till the end of time...

"Echoes of Strength:
A Symphony of Shared Lives"

In the echoes of her past, a tale unfolds,
A narrative of strength, in silence it molds.
Through the trials, alone she trod,
My heart now heavy, soaked in pain's abode.

Guilt weaves its threads within my core,
For absent I stood in moments she bore.
No solace offered, no hand to clasp,
As shadows of hardship cast a lasting grasp.

Dreams once vivid now shrouded in night,
Lost in the abyss, out of sight.
Darkness engulfs with each passing day,
A relentless tide, dragging me away.

To support her now, my sole decree,
In whatever form, however free.
Her happiness, my reason to live,
All of myself, to her, I give.

No remnants left that I can claim,
Merged with her, love the only flame.
Her pain eclipses my hollow strife,
Lost within the tapestry of her life.

No selfish want, no personal plea,
Only to be the anchor, sturdy and free.
A life entwined in shared memories,
A canvas painted with love's treasuries.

Emptiness within, a small cost to bear,
Her burdens heavier, harder to wear.
Yet, in this shared journey, I find,
A purpose true, in love enshrined.

A life with her, a tapestry divine,
Where moments are woven, hearts entwine.
I'll hold her close, through joy and grime,
Bound to her, till the end of time.

"Love's Surrender:
A Poetic Farewell"

Now even the soft rub is not in the stars,
As my heart has gone on some personal wars,
With the gist of your smile, I'll close my eyes,
This is the truth,maybe my love is a lie,
Because the true affection doesnt have a fate,
Am losing myself with every passing date.
Your time with me has now come to a phase,
Where you anymore, i won't chase.
Now i want to sleep so deep,that i wont wake up anymore,
This heart is tearing apart ,and the body so sore.
This last gift of mine, which is a stress free life,
I want to give it to you , with all my strength and strife
& then I'll find a path, where i could either die deep in sea
Or bury in a ground somewhere, where you couldn't see
As i have accepted that i have lost you in this birth,
And i want to cross down to the next, for holding your girth
With all the memories ill close my eyes someday and sometime
Because I'll forever love you,
Till the end of time...

"Love's Dawn:
A Tapestry of Yearning"

In the dawn's tender light, a love so pure,
Each day blooms with affection, of that I'm sure.
Through all my silly deeds, you see my heart,
A tapestry of emotions, a passionate art.

Your hand in mine, a cherished craving,
The creases intertwine, in warmth, behaving.
My palms unfold, seeking your gentle touch,
A thirst in my chest, for love's sweet clutch.

In the twilight's embrace, I yearn to hold,
To submerge you in my arms, a tale untold.
With each waking moment, you're not there,
I long for your gaze, the answer to my prayer.

In the morning's first light, and as night descends,
I yearn for you, my love, my dearest friend.
To kiss you gently, to make your lips blush,
Unveiling that smile, in a tender hush.

Your smile, a canvas of beauty, so divine,
I want to be the reason, the spark that'll shine.
I open my eyes, seeking you every morn,
You're the last thought, as the day is worn.

I'll wait for you, through the rivers of time,
A love so enduring, a rhythm, a rhyme.
Until you feel the depth of my love's chime,
I'll wait, my dear, till the end of time.

"Symphony of Solitude:
A Love Etched in Time"

In the silent symphony of solitude, missing you becomes my breath,
An involuntary rhythm, a dance of life and death.
Your touch, a memory etched in the echoes of air,
Fingers ache to traverse the silk of your hair.

Cravings born in the quiet of night,
To cocoon you in calmness, hold you tight.
My life, a canvas, painted in hues of your delight,
Surrendered to your happiness, a vow, a silent rite.

Together or apart, the "us" we create,
A fate entwined, an unspoken soulmate.
Your arms, my sanctuary, a refuge so divine,
Home, peace, calmness—a haven that's mine.

Your smile, a sunrise in the darkest of skies,
A radiant beacon that bids sorrow goodbye.
I sculpt it with laughter, with every joyous tease,
To keep it beautiful, a masterpiece that frees.

Adoration, a river that time can't confine,
Each day, a testament, a love intertwine.
I adore you in daylight, in shadows profound,
Missing you's a heartbeat, a perpetual sound.

Each day, a promise etched in the sun's golden ray,
To love, to miss, to cherish, come what may.
Till the end of time, a vow profound,
In the tapestry of eternity, our love is bound.

"Echoes of Love:
Navigating the Tapestry of Time"

In the shadows of each passing day,
I miss you in the silence, as words decay.
Our endless conversations, once so sweet,
Now lost in the echoes, where memories meet.

I wonder where we've gone astray,
Distances growing, love slipping away.
Yearning for the you I used to adore,
The one who had my time, forevermore.

In the tapestry of time, threads entwined,
I seek the version of you, now hard to find.
Craving for the warmth we used to share,
A soulful connection, beyond compare.

Time, a subtle thief, has stolen grace,
Altered the contours of your familiar face.
I don't know if it's fate or my own mistake,
But I long for the you, I can't forsake.

Somewhere in the whispers of the wind,
I sense a changed you, a subtle spin.
Yet, my heart holds on to the you I knew,
A quest to find the essence that once grew.

Lost in the maze of moments gone by,
I search for the truth, beneath the sky.
You, different now, yet my heart's decree,
Forever etched in its chambers, undeniably.

Maybe time has sculpted a different art,
But I'll keep looking for the missing part.
My heart whispers, "Wait, don't despair,"
For the you I'll find, the one so rare.

Till the end of time, my love will persist,
In the echoes of memories, love will persist.
I'll wait for the you, lost but not gone,
In the symphony of time, love lingers on.

"Eternal Threads:
Love's Tapestry Unfolds"

In the tapestry of time, I patiently stand,
A silent witness to the dance of fate's hand.
In the shadows I linger, a love untold,
For you, my heart's secret, a tale to unfold.

I'll wait for the stars to align in the night,
To reveal my affection, pure and bright.
Within my arms, a haven for your soul,
Where happiness thrives and love takes control.

Yet these distances between us, a test,
To build trust, to kindle what's best.
I'll wait for the day you see and believe,
My love for you, unwavering, like autumn leaves.

You may forget me like a fleeting dream,
In the morning light, lost in the sunbeam.
But in the clouds of life, if you disappear,
I'll hold onto the echoes of you, crystal clear.

In the deep waters where darkness resides,
I'll remember you, where my heart abides.
Every second, every moment, you're there,
A constant, like breathing in the open air.

As time unfolds, memories may fade,
But my love for you will never degrade.
Your smile, a sunrise in my darkest night,
Guiding me through the labyrinth, towards the light.

You are my life, my joy, my forever,
In your absence, I'll endeavour.
To hold onto the threads of our story,
I'll always weave my love's never-ending glory.

"Starlit Serenade:
Tales from the Night Drive"

In the quiet hum of the moving car,
Beside her, I find my world, my star.
She hugs her bag in a cozy embrace,
Sleeping, leaning on the window with grace.

Sideways I glimpse her angelic face,
Streetlight flashes, a radiant trace.
Dark to light, a mesmerizing play,
Her lips and cheeks, a love display.

Curly strands hiding eyes so deep,
A beauty words fail to keep.
Her elegance, a timeless art,
Captures my soul, ensnares my heart.

I yearn to kiss those lips so sweet,
Hold her hand, our fingers meet.
Yet, she sleeps like a child so divine,
My Sleeping Beauty, forever mine.

Home approaches, the journey ends,
I wake her gently, my love transcends.
Slowly, her eyes open and meet mine,
A moment cherished, forever in time.

In the hushed embrace of the night,
Our silent love takes its flight.
A memory etched, a love sublime,
Forever I'll love her, till the end of time.

"Melody of Regret:
A Love Unspoken"

In shadows deep, where love once thrived,
A tale of hearts, but fate contrived.
I gaze upon her, my love untold,
A story written yet left unsold.

Her name a melody, sweet and divine,
In every verse, in every line.
Yet, in the echoes of our shared delight,
Lies a truth that dims love's shining light.

For she, my love, desires a path apart,
A choice that tears at this devoted heart.
I've realized, accepted, in solitude's embrace,
Our love may falter, a fleeting grace.

To leave this world, her image in my mind,
A choice that seems to fate, unkind.
I can't trust anew, love another soul,
For in her absence, a void takes its toll.

She's the sun that warms my every day,
Yet, our love, she wishes to cast away.
I don't want to be anyone but me,
Bound to a love that couldn't truly be.

In her absence, a lingering regret,
A love unfulfilled, a soul beset.
Cheeku, my endearing, cherished one,
I'll forever mourn the love undone.

Guilt shall linger in the spaces between,
A love story, untold, yet keen.
I depart, leaving love behind,
A bittersweet ache, in my heart confined.

To miss her always, in the tapestry of time,
A departure written in a melancholy rhyme.
Farewell, my love, in shadows I'll grieve,
For a love unspoken, yet boundless, I leave.

www.ingramcontent.com/pod-product-compliance
Lightning Source LLC
LaVergne TN
LVHW061548070526
838199LV00077B/6957